Liturgical Reflections

Liturgical Reflections

of a Papal Master of Ceremonies

Reverend Monsignor
GUIDO MARINI

Translated by
Reverend Nicholas L. Gregoris

NEWMAN HOUSE PRESS

Liturgical Reflections of a Papal Master of Ceremonies

ISBN 978-0-9778846-5-0

Printed in the United States of America

Contents

Publisher's Preface   7

Foreword   11

Holy Communion   45

The Pallium   51

The Staff   59

The Crucifix   65

The Greek Gospel   71

Silence   83

Latin   89

Beauty   95

The Dalmatic   103

Notes   111

Publisher's Preface

Anyone who watches or participates in a papal liturgy is struck by the seeming effortlessness with which it is conducted, resulting in a celebration which is prayerful, dignified, and uplifting. Of course, as anyone might also surmise, such an achievement is not possible without great effort – study, prayer, reflection, rehearsal. The person responsible for bringing the many elements together (liturgical texts, music, ministers, worship aids for the congregation, the Pope himself) is the priest designated as the "Master of Pontifical Ceremonies." He is discretely omnipresent, always found standing to the left of the Sovereign Pontiff. For some time now, that man has been the Reverend Monsignor Guido Marini, a priest of the Archdiocese of Genoa, known for his gentleness and clear vision.

Since assuming this role, Monsignor Marini has taken opportunities to explain why he makes the liturgical judgments he makes and how they are grounded in both sound thelogical principles and the goals of Pope Benedict XVI for the liturgical life of the whole Church. Monsignor Marini has also taken to publishing on the Holy See's Website short articles providing background on various aspects of the pontifical ceremonies. It has been a pleasure for the Reverend Nicholas L. Gregoris and me to assist in the production of the English translations of the original Italian texts. With the positive reception accorded these insightful essays, Father Gregoris and I approached Monsignor Marini with the proposal of assembling these texts into one volume and publishing them for the benefit of the English-speaking Catholic world – to which Monsignor Marini graciously consented.

One can ask, however, "Of what value are the reflections of a Master of Pontifical Ceremonies?" From time immemorial, the way the Bishop of Rome has celebrated the Sacred Liturgy has been normative for the Roman Rite. Although the Pope can surely legislate on liturgical matters, he likewise serves as a liturgical "pace-setter," offering a standard by which all can judge their own liturgies. What the Pope does in the sacred rites has taken on even greater importance in the present age of easy communication and travel, making papal ceremonies even more accessible and thus, potentially, even more exemplary. In the behind-the-scene planning for those ceremonies, the Master of Pontifical Ceremonies has a unique role; and the autonomy and competence of the Office of Pontifical Celebrations of the Supreme Pontiff within the Roman Curia were confirmed by legislation in 1981 and 1995.

How does Monsignor Marini regard his mission? In one of his own essays, he provides this answer: .

"faithful interpreter and echo of [the Pope's] authoritative liturgical orientation, which does not pertain to the realm of 'personal taste'. . . but rather to a true and proper Magisterium to be shared with a spirit of faith and a genuine ecclesial sense." And what influence does, or should, this mission have on the whole Church? Cardinal Antonio Cañizares-Llovera, Prefect of the Congregation for Divine Worship and the Discipline of the Sacraments, spoke on this topic in an interview he gave to the Italian magazine *Trenta Giorni* (March 2009): ". . . take to heart how the Holy Father – assisted by the Office headed by Monsignor Guido Marini – celebrates the liturgy. The papal Liturgy in fact have always been, and still are, exemplary for the whole Catholic world." What the Pope does should be emulated by all priests of the Roman Rite.

I am grateful to Monsignor Marini for allowing us to disseminate these reflections; and to Father Gregoris for his careful translation. By giving priests and laity alike this access to the thought of the Holy Father, Benedict XVI, his liturgical practice can sooner become the model for theirs.

Reverend Peter M. J. Stravinskas
General Editor and Publisher
NEWMAN HOUSE PRESS

FOREWORD

Entering the Liturgical Mysteries through the Rites and Prayers

ADDRESS TO LITURGY CONFERENCE
Mileto, 6–7 September 2010

———

". . . through a good understanding of the rites and prayers they should take part in the sacred action conscious of what they are doing, with devotion and full collaboration."

— *Sacrosanctum Concilium*, no. 48

It seems proper to me that there could not be a title that better expresses one of the elements which describes the liturgy in a major way and which, together, picks up a fundamental orientation from the Constitution on the Sacred Liturgy of the Second Vatican Council.

In effect, it is precisely about this topic that we speak when speaking of the liturgy: the collection of rites and prayers through which we are able to have access to the mystery of Christ, given to us through the Church.

Therefore, it is worth the effort to reflect calmly on each of the expressions contained in the title of the conference entrusted to me, during which I intend to make frequent references to the theological

13

thought of Cardinal Ratzinger and to the Magisterium of Pope Benedict XVI, above all because I consider it a pleasant and urgent duty for me to be the faithful interpreter and echo of his authoritative liturgical orientation, which does not pertain to the realm of "personal taste" (although such personal taste is more than respected while not necessarily shared by all), but rather to a true and proper Magisterium to be shared with a spirit of faith and a genuine ecclesial sense.

1. "The Mystery That Is Celebrated"

The actual presence of our salvation

We know very well that in the liturgy the mystery of our salvation is made present in a sacramental way. He Who is risen from the dead, the Living One, renews His redemptive sacrifice through the power of the Holy Spirit. "Who, therefore, saves the world and man? The only answer we can give is: Jesus of Nazareth, Lord and Christ, Crucified and Risen," affirmed Pope Benedict recently. "And where is the Mystery of the Death and Resurrection of Christ that brings about salvation? In Christ's action through the Church, and in particular in the Sacrament of the Eucharist, which makes the redemptive sacrificial offering of the Son of God present. . . ." [1]

The liturgy, therefore, is not something we remember but which time has relegated to a past left behind forever. Nor does it deal with an assemblage of rites, purely esthetically lovely, but bereft of life and incapable of communicating salvation. Nor does it deal with a mere assembly of persons who share an ideal and intend to form a community. Rather, the liturgy deals with a celebration by which we truly enter into a relationship with the mystery of our salvation, with Christ the Lord, the Savior, Who communicates His very own life to us – His grace. Thus the past is rendered present, the beautiful truly manifests the beauty of the Living God, and new fraternal relations are the fruit of the work of the Lord in the heart of man.

In my view, it is essential that every Christian generation renew the perception of faith concerning such a reality, that is to say, of a celebration that is truly the means by which an encounter with the Lord takes place in the "today" of our life and history. It always strikes me how much the most experienced guides say to the visitors of the Basilica of Saint Peter's in Rome, when they stop to contemplate Michelangelo's masterpiece, the *Pietà*. As you know, the work of this great artist is located where preparations are currently made for the Eucharistic celebration whenever the Holy Father is present. Thus, the guides point out that the hands of the Madonna are open almost as if wanting to hand over the sacrificed Body of Jesus to the onlooker. The *Pietà* was created by Michelangelo as a frontal for an altar and, therefore, was destined to be the background for the altar of the Eucharistic celebration. In this way, the celebrant and the entire assembly would be able to contemplate the gesture of the Most Holy Virgin, in the act of giving the Savior to the Church during the Eucharistic celebration. How beautiful to recall this artistic detail! In the celebration of the Mass, the Risen Lord, through His Word, in His Body and Blood, gives Himself to us, so that we can enter into the mystery of His life, and thus be saved.

Permit me, by the way, to call your attention to another artistic detail of the splendid Basilica of Saint Peter. The baldacchino that stands above the great altar of the *confessio* is the work of Bernini. If we observe carefully the drapery that covers the high part of the baldacchino, we can note that the design does not appear static but rather capable of giving a clear impression of dynamism. In other words, it seems that that drapery could be moved by a gust of wind – as delicate as it is imposing.

In this way, Bernini intended to underscore what takes place at the moment of the Eucharistic Prayer, and, in particular, at the moment of the consecration: the Holy Spirit truly descends upon the altar of Eucharistic celebration and is the Creator, together with the words and actions of Christ, of the substantial transformation or "transubstantiation" of the bread and wine into the Body and Blood of the Lord (see *Catechism of the Catholic Church*, no. 1353). The Spirit, Who is the Giver of Life, makes truly present the Risen Lord in the act of His redemptive sacrifice. And so, expressed in art is the reality of the mystery that is celebrated. Here and now, the Savior is present and acting in His mystery of love and of grace. John Paul II said: "Since the liturgy is the exercise of the priesthood of Christ, it is necessary to keep ever alive the affirmation of the disciple faced with the mysterious presence of the Lord: 'It is the Lord!'(Jn 21:7). Nothing of what we do in the liturgy can appear more important than what in an unseen but real manner Christ accomplishes by the power of His Spirit."[2] This truth of liturgical action must always be at the center of the faith-awareness of those who participate in the liturgical celebration.

The Sacred Mystery

I will now reflect for a moment on the word "mystery." It is clear that by using this term we do not intend something obscure, esoteric, and disquieting. Rather, we intend to highlight the salvific work of God, Whose light is so illuminating, although never making it completely comprehensible to man; the human person must, at a certain point along the way, leave room for faith in order to have access to the One Who is Truth. As we usually say, it is precisely such salvific work that is celebrated in the liturgy. Therefore, it is not the work of man that has primacy in the Eucharistic celebration but the work of God, the paschal event of the Lord's Death and Resurrection. We do not want to misunderstand the importance of man's work in the liturgy, but to put in proper perspective the relationship of the necessary dependence of human action on that of the Lord's own action.

In this regard, Benedict XVI gave the following explanation when addressing the bishops of the Brazilian Episcopal Conference during their *ad limina* visit:

"Now, the main, fundamental attitude of the Christian faithful who take part in the liturgical celebration is not action but listening, opening themselves, receiving. . . . It is clear that in this case receiving does not mean remaining passive or uninterested in what is going on there but cooperating since by God's grace they are once again enabled to do so in accordance with 'the real nature of the true Church. The Church is essentially both human and divine, visible but endowed with invisible realties, zealous in action and dedicated to contemplation, present in the world, but as a pilgrim, so constituted that in her the human is directed toward and subordinated to the divine, the visible to the invisible, action to contemplation, and this present world to that city yet to come, the object of our quest' (*Sacrosanctum Concilium*, no. 2). If in the liturgy, the figure of Christ, Who is its principle and is really present to make it effective, were not to emerge we should no longer have the Christian liturgy, completely dependent upon the Lord and sustained by His creative presence."[3]

For this reason, it is necessary to join the term "sacred" to the term "mystery." To affirm the "sacrality" of the liturgy means to remember the necessity of safeguarding with care the mystery that is being celebrated in the liturgy. Liturgical sacrality is the objectivity of the mystery that, time after time, does not cease to interest man — inasmuch as it gives man what he really needs and saves him, permitting him to enter into true joy.

In this sense, the acceptance of the mystery in view of personal transformation and conversion is the principal act to which we are called in the celebration of the liturgy. This is, if we want to call it such, the most authentic creativity that ought to characterize the life of the individual believer and of the celebrating community. Other types of creativity, when not envisioned by the rite itself and which we can easily describe as terribly detracting from the truth of the Eucharistic celebration, only run the risk of being the expression of a celebration of oneself as an individual or as a particular community. These forms of creativity lose sight of the primary subject of the liturgy, Who is God.

In Cardinal Ratzinger's address to the Chilean

Episcopal Conference on 3 July 1988, he made the following explanation in this regard:

"We ought to get back the dimension of the sacred in the liturgy. The liturgy is not a festivity; it is not a meeting for the purpose of having a good time. It is of no importance that the parish priest has cudgeled his brains to come up with suggestive ideas or imaginative novelties. The liturgy is what makes the Thrice-Holy God present amongst us; it is the burning bush; it is the Alliance of God with man in Jesus Christ, Who has died and risen again. The grandeur of the liturgy does not rest upon the fact that it offers an interesting entertainment, but in rendering tangible the Totally Other, Whom we are not capable of summoning. He comes because He wills. In other words, the essential in the liturgy is the mystery, which is realized in the common ritual of the Church; all the rest diminishes it. Men experiment with it in lively fashion, and find themselves deceived, when the mystery is transformed into distraction, when the chief actor in the liturgy is not the Living God but the priest or the liturgical director.

"In this context, we should not underestimate the inherent question of liturgical rubrics and, more generally speaking, the norms regarding the liturgy. The liturgical norms, in fact, serve as the closest guardian of the mystery being celebrated. The rubrics affirm and equally guarantee ritual unity and, consequently, are capable of giving expression to the catholicity of the Church's liturgy. At the same time, norms serve as a vehicle for liturgical and doctrinal content that a centuries-old tradition and proven experience have transmitted to us and which it is wrong to treat with superficiality and to pollute with our poor and limited subjectivity. Herein lies the foundation of this observation that time and again has been re-proposed by the papal Magisterium, past and present. 'Since liturgical celebrations are not private acts but "celebrations of the Church, the sacrament of unity,"' affirmed John Paul II, 'their regulation is dependent solely upon the hierarchical authority of the Church. The liturgy belongs to the whole body of the Church. It is for this reason that it is not permitted to anyone, even the priest, or any group, to subtract or change anything whatsoever on their own initiative.'"[4]

"Holy Mass, celebrated with respect for the liturgical norms and with appropriate appreciation of the riches of the signs and gestures," affirmed Benedict XVI, "encourages and develops growth in Eucharistic faith."

He continues:

"In the Eucharistic celebration we do not invent something but rather enter into a reality that precedes us, indeed that embraces Heaven and earth and therefore also past, future and present. This universal openness, this encounter with all God's sons and daughters is the greatness of the Eucharist: Let us go to meet the reality of God present among us in the Body and Blood of the Risen One. Therefore, the liturgical prescriptions dictated by the Church are not external appendices but express in practice this reality of the revelation of Christ's Body and Blood, and thus prayer reveals faith, according to the ancient principle *lex orandi, lex credendi*. And for this reason, we can say that 'the best catechesis on the Eucharist is the Eucharist itself, celebrated well'" (*Sacramentum Caritatis*, no. 64).[5]

Therefore, it is necessary to have an attitude that is balanced, capable of maintaining as complementary and necessary the ritual and symbolic perspective, as well as the canonical and disciplinary perspective – not one perspective without the other, but the one with the other.

2. "To enter"

The meaning of the verb

The verb "to enter," chosen as part of my title for this talk, is an important verb because it also leads us to the major theme of participation in the liturgical celebration – a theme that impassions and inspires us and that at times leads to discussions which, in my opinion, also lead to useless polemics and divisions. Who among us, in fact, does not desire the liturgy to be truly participated in by everyone? Above all, from the time of *Sacrosanctum Concilium*, and thereafter, hasn't the reform begun by the Second Vatican Council and continued by later papal Magisterium rightly insisted on the most ample and authentic realization of such participation? On the other hand, if the life of the Church and the encounter of every man with Christ the Savior is something dear to everyone's heart, can we not perhaps desire that all participate in the Sacred Liturgy with the greatest possible benefit?

Therefore, on this score, I would say that it would be difficult to have divergent opinions. The disparity of views can take place when we seek to specify better what we mean by participation, or what would be more adequate ways needed for entering into the mystery being celebrated. And we know, as far as this is concerned, how two diverse ways of considering the term "enter" often continue to be contrasted. As always in Catholic doctrine, so too in this case, there is no room for *aut/aut* (either/or), or for the exclusion of one aspect in favor of another aspect, but for *et/et* (both/and), or for the complementary and enriching presence of different aspects.

To enter into a reality, to participate in an event is always an experience that involves man in his every dimension: intellect, will, emotion, sentiment, action, etcetera. The external nature of action and its interior foundation result as complementary and necessary. And so it is for the liturgical life, precisely because life's experience must be concerned with the whole complexity of the human person. For example, if there is participation that comes about by means of comprehending a text, it is also a form of participation that occurs when the soul is uplifted as it encounters the beautiful. And as the soul participates by means of action, it is also possible to realize a true participation by means of silence — which only appears to be inactive.

Consequently, in the mystery being celebrated, we enter with the entire complexity of our human persons. And this is why the liturgy always seeks that healthy equilibrium of components that would afford the possibility of an experience that belongs to the whole of man and to every man.

It seems to me that this does not always find a happy and balanced realization in liturgical practice. And it also seems to me that, according to the law of the pendulum, if at one time the lack of adequate participation may have been caused by a defect in understanding and action, today such a lack of adequate participation may be caused by an excess of rational comprehension and external action, to which there is not always present a sufficient and complementary understanding of the heart and attention to the interior action, so as to re-live in oneself the sentiments and thoughts of Christ.

To enter into the action of Christ

Now let us go a little deeper into the question, starting from the direction clearly formulated by the Constitution on the Sacred Liturgy of the Second Vatican Council:

"The Church, therefore, earnestly desires that Christ's faithful, when present at this mystery of faith, should not be there as strangers or silent spectators; on the contrary, through a good understanding of the rites and prayers they should take part in the sacred action conscious of what they are doing, with devotion and full collaboration. They should be instructed by God's Word and be nourished at the table of the Lord's Body; they should give thanks to God; by offering the Immaculate Victim, not only through the hands of the priest, but also with him, they should learn also to offer themselves; through Christ the Mediator, they should be drawn day by day into ever more perfect union with God and with each other, so that finally God may be all in all" (no. 48).

As a way of commenting on this always illuminating magisterial passage, Cardinal Ratzinger affirmed in his book *The Spirit of the liturgy*:

"But what does the active participation come down to? What does it mean that we have to do? Unfortunately, the word was very quickly misunderstood to mean something external, entailing a need for general activity, as if as many people as possible, as often as possible, should be visibly engaged in action. However, the word 'part-icipation' refers to a principal action in which everyone has a 'part.' And so, if we want to discover the kind of doing that active participation involves, we need, first of all, to determine what this central *actio* is in which all the members of the community are supposed to participate. The study of the liturgical sources provides an answer that at first may surprise us, though, in the light of the biblical foundations considered in the first part, it is quite self-evident. By the *actio* of the liturgy the sources mean the Eucharistic Prayer. The real liturgical action, the true liturgical act, is the *oratio*. . . . This *oratio* – the Eucharistic Prayer, the 'Canon' – is really more than speech; it is *actio* in the highest sense of the word. For what happens in it is that the human *actio* . . . steps back and makes way for the *actio divina*, the action of God." [6]

In the liturgical celebration what precedes and constitutes the foundation is the action of Christ and of His Church; in fact, as Pope John Paul II recalled, "Since Christ's Death on the Cross and His Resurrection constitute the content of the daily life of the Church and the pledge of His eternal Passover, the liturgy has as its first task to lead us untiringly back to the Easter pilgrimage initiated by Christ, in which we accept death in order to enter into life." [7] Consequently, to enter into the liturgical act means entering into the action that confers salvation and transforms life. We participate, therefore, to the extent that the action of the Lord and of His Church also becomes our action, His oblation of love becomes our oblation of love, His filial and obedient abandonment to the Father becomes ours as well – if the Sacrifice of the Redeemer becomes our own sacrifice.

Divo Barsotti affirms in his celebrated text:

"It truly pertains to the Christian liturgy to transcend the activity of every man and of every activity of humanity by being the Act of Christ Himself. However, the liturgy transcends every human activity without excluding it, engaging it fully and profoundly, not only insofar as the liturgy transcends the human activity, but also in that it requires and comprehends the human activity."[8]

As always happens in what is human, so too in the liturgical rite, action has both an external and an internal dimension. The gesture of Christ is a visible gesture that expresses an invisible reality. Moreover, the act of entering into the mystery will undoubtedly possess an external gesture as a component. But since such a component does not remain purely a sterile form of externalism, it will have to be enlivened and at the same time lead to that interior action in which there is conformity to the action of Christ and of His Church.

Therefore, space should be given to external action in the liturgy, where the rite permits it and makes it auspicious – but without forgetting that such action will always have to be redirected to its correct expression of interior action. Only in that way will there be authentic access to the mystery that is celebrated.

3. "Through Rites and Prayers"

What has been said about entering into the mystery has had a general character to it. Now, by mentioning rites and prayers, the title of the talk allows us to enter into a more specific realm, or into the typical mode of the liturgy to make accessible the participation of the mystery being celebrated.

Rites and prayers in the liturgy are sustained by each other and enlighten one another, precisely so as to make the celebration come alive. The rite would remain deprived of light without the prayer that enlightens it; the prayer would remain deprived of efficacy without the rite that puts it into action. Furthermore, the liturgical celebration demands that type of faith which remains neither extraneous to prayer nor extraneous to the rite.

With good reason has the tradition of the Church always held in great esteem the famous catecheses of the ancient Fathers of the Church – catecheses which, going back to the prayers and rites, introduce the faithful to the knowledge and experience of the mystery being celebrated. At the present time, we recognize the great need for such catecheses. In fact, presenting Christian culture as esoteric to very young people and very broadly within the social context leads to a serious form of "ignorance" with respect to the rites and prayers of the liturgy. And we cannot ask of the liturgy what it cannot give — catechesis. Undoubtedly, the liturgy is learned by living it; however, a type of catechesis is necessary that is also a movement toward liturgical experience, serving as an introduction to the divine mysteries.

It seems to me that the same task that was thought urgent at the time of the Second Vatican Council has remained urgent to the present time, perhaps with a sense of greater urgency — the need for formation. Only thanks to a true liturgical formation will the rites and prayers of the celebration be able to serve as a beautiful and extraordinarily rich vehicle for entering into the mystery being celebrated. Otherwise, we risk remaining at the threshold of an inaccessible reality.

On the other hand, it is good to remember that the liturgical celebration realized according to the truth and in conformity with the *ars celebrandi* (art of celebrating) of which the Holy Father, Benedict XVI, speaks to us in his apostolic exhortation *Sacramentum Caritatis*, or in full conformity with the norms of the Church, is already *per se* a true and proper school, capable of leading to knowledge and experience of the mystery of Christ. Therefore, rites and prayers celebrated well are an authentic introduction to the spirit of the liturgy.

It is not, however, my intention to enter into the details of the rites and prayers, insofar as I would like to focus my consideration on certain aspects of the acts of the liturgical celebration that help us to enter into the Sacred Liturgy, into its rites and prayers. The aspects that will be considered will be only a handful – those that seem to me more important and urgent to underscore and to explain in the present historical context. It is not my intention thereby to diminish the importance of other aspects, but we cannot say everything and it is necessary to provide a certain priority.

Sacred Silence

A well-celebrated liturgy, in its various parts, provides for a happy alternation of silence and the spoken word, as silence gives life to the word, permitting the voice to resound with extraordinary profundity, maintaining every vocal expression in the right climate of recollection. We recall in this regard the affirmation found in the General Instruction of the Roman Missal:

"Sacred silence also, as part of the celebration, is to be observed at the designated times. Its purpose, however, depends on the time it occurs in each part of the celebration. Thus within the Act of Penitence and again after the invitation to pray, all recollect themselves; but at the conclusion of a reading or the homily, all meditate briefly on what they have heard; then after Communion, they praise and pray to God in their hearts" (no. 45).

The General Instruction does nothing more than make explicit what *Sacrosanctum Concilium* formulated in general terms: ". . . at the proper times all should observe a reverent silence" (no. 30).

It should be noted that, in both texts just cited, "sacred silence" is mentioned. The silence requested, moreover, is not to be considered along the lines of a mere pause between one moment of celebration and another that follows. Rather, it is to be considered a true and proper ritual moment, complementary to the proclamation of the Word, to vocal prayer, to song, to gesture, and so on.

From this point of view, we can better understand why during the Liturgy of the Eucharist and, in particular, during the Canon, the People of God, united in prayer, follow in silence the prayer of the priest-celebrant. That silence does not mean being inactive or lacking participation. That silence is intended to allow everyone to enter into the significance of that ritual moment which renews in the reality of the sacrament the act of love with which Jesus offers Himself to the Father on the Cross for the salvation of the world. That silence, truly sacred, is the liturgical space in which to say "yes" to the action of Christ with all the strength of our being, so that the action of Christ becomes our very own in daily life.

Thus, liturgical silence is truly sacred because it is the spiritual place to realize the adherence of our whole life to the life of the Lord; it is the space of the prolonged "amen" of the heart surrendering to the love of God and embracing that love as a new criterion of our own existence. Is this not perhaps the stupendous significance of the "amen" that concludes the doxology at the end of the Eucharistic Prayer, in which we vocalize what for such a long time we have been repeating in the silence of our hearts rapt in prayer?

If all this is the meaning of silence in the liturgy, is it not perhaps true that our liturgies are in need of more room for sacred silence?

Noble Beauty

Pope Benedict XVI affirms in *Sacramentum Caritatis*:

"This relationship between creed and worship is evidenced in a particular way by the rich theological and liturgical category of beauty. Like the rest of Christian Revelation, the liturgy is inherently linked to beauty: it is *veritatis splendor*. . . . This is no mere aestheticism, but the concrete way in which the truth of God's love in Christ encounters us, attracts us and delights us, enabling us to emerge from ourselves and drawing us towards our true vocation, which is love. The truest beauty is the love of God,

Who definitively revealed Himself to us in the paschal mystery. . . . Beauty, then, is not mere decoration, but rather an essential element of the liturgical action, since it is an attribute of God Himself and His revelation. These considerations should make us realize the care which is needed, if the liturgical action is to reflect its innate splendor" (no. 35).

The words of the Pope could not be clearer. It follows from them that no form of stinginess is admissible, nor any type of minimalism and of ill-intentioned impoverishment in the liturgical celebration. The beautiful, in its diverse ancient and modern forms in which it finds expression, is the proper means by which the mystery of the beauty of the love of God shines forth in our liturgies, even if always but dimly. Hence, why we can never do enough to beautify our rites! The Church teaches us that, in her long history, she has never feared to "waste" in order to surround the liturgical celebration with the highest expressions of art: from architecture to sculpture, to music, to sacred objects. The saints, despite their personal poverty, have always taught us to desire that only the best things be set aside for divine worship.

Once again, let us listen to Benedict XVI:

"Our earthly liturgies, entirely ordered to the celebration of this unique act within history, will never fully express its infinite meaning. Certainly, the beauty of our celebrations can never be sufficiently cultivated, fostered and refined, for nothing can be too beautiful for God, Who is Himself infinite Beauty. Yet our earthly liturgies will never be more than a pale reflection of the liturgy celebrated in the Jerusalem on high, the goal of our pilgrimage on earth. May our own celebrations nonetheless resemble that liturgy as closely as possible and grant us a foretaste of it!" [9]

The Crucifix at the Center of the Altar

In Cardinal Ratzinger's book *Feast of Faith*, which was first published in 1981, he presented the problem of the orientation of the altar in the context of the liturgical celebration. To cite here some passages of his text seems to me to be the most immediate way to understand the importance of his reflection and his proposal:

"For the true location and the true context of the Eucharistic celebration is the whole cosmos. 'Facing east' makes the cosmic dimension of the Eucharist present through liturgical gesture. Because of the rising of the sun, the east – *oriens* – was naturally both a symbol of the Resurrection (and to that extent it was not merely a Christological statement but also a reminder of the Father's power and the influence of the Holy Spirit) and a presentation of the hope of the Parousia. . . . So, what has come down to us in the altar cross is a relic of the ancient eastward orientation. It maintained the ancient tradition of praying to the Lord Who is to come under the sign of the cross, a tradition with strong associations, in former times, with the cosmic symbol of the 'east.' . . . Even now, when the priest faces the people, the cross could be placed on the altar in such a way that both priest and people can see it. At the Eucharistic Prayer they should not look at one another; together they ought to behold Him, the Pierced Savior (Zech 12:10; Rev 1:7). . . . But the cross on the altar is not obstructing the view; it is the common point of reference. . . . I would even be so bold as to suggest that the cross on the altar is actually a necessary precondition for celebrating toward the people. It would help in clarifying the distinction between the Liturgy of the Word and the Liturgy of the Eucharist. The first is concerned with proclamation and hence with a direct, face-to-face situation, whereas the second is a matter of all of us worshiping together in response to the call *Conversi ad Dominum* — Let us turn to the Lord; let us be converted to the Lord!" [10]

In light of these clear affirmations, we understand better what is underscored by the Holy Father, Benedict XVI, in the Preface to the first volume of his Collected Works (*Opera Omnia*), dedicated to the liturgy and only recently released in Italy:

"The idea that priest and people must look at each other in prayer is a novelty of modern Christianity and is completely foreign to ancient Christianity. Priest and people certainly do not pray facing one other, but facing the one Lord. Therefore, during prayer they look in the same direction: or toward the East as a cosmic symbol in expectation of the Lord Who is coming, or, where this is not possible, toward an image of Christ in the apse, toward a cross, or simply toward Heaven, as the Lord did in His High Priestly Prayer on the night before His Passion (Jn 17:1). In the meantime, the proposal I made at the end of the chapter about this topic in my work *The Spirit of the Liturgy* (pp. 83–84) is steadily making progress, namely, not to make any new changes, but simply to place the cross at the center of the altar, toward which the priest and faithful can look together, thus allowing themselves to be guided toward the Lord, Whom we beseech all together."

Adoration

What do we mean by adoration? Certainly, it does not mean an intellectual or sentimental relationship to the mystery. Adoration could be defined as the full recognition of wonder before the omnipotence of God, of His intangible majesty, of His provident and merciful Lordship, of His infinite beauty that is the coming together of truth and love. And adoration, when it is authentic, leads to adherence or to the reunification of man and creation with God, to man's exit from a state of separation from God toward a communion of life with Christ. All this is what the Church, the Spouse of Christ, experiences in the celebration of the liturgy. Adore and adhere, adore so that you may adhere to Christ.

Let us listen once again to Divo Barsotti in his already cited work:

"And the Event, the Act of Christ, is first and foremost a Sacrifice, a Sacrifice of Adoration. The Word, in the human nature He assumed, acknowledges with His death the infinite holiness of God and His sovereignty. In Him creation finally adores. . . . Our participation in the Sacrifice of Jesus requires that we undergo the same self-emptying as He. The earthly condition of our life, in its voluntary acceptance, becomes the sign of our participation in the Sacrifice of Jesus and in His adoration." [11]

And so, everything in the liturgical action must lead to adoration: the music, the chant, the silence, the way of proclaiming the Word of God and of praying, the gestures, the liturgical vestments and sacred vessels; likewise, too, the entire complex of the sacred edifice should lead us to adoration. For a moment, I would like to focus on a gesture that is typical and central to adoration, and one that today runs the risk of disappearing, namely, kneeling. I make reference here to a text of Cardinal Ratzinger:

"We know that the Lord prayed remaining on His

knees (Lk 22:41), that Stephen (Acts 7:60), Peter (Acts 9:40) and Paul (Acts 20:36) prayed on their knees. The Christological hymn of the Letter to the Philippians (2:6–11) presents the liturgy of the cosmos as a bending of the knee at the name of Jesus (2:10) and sees in it a fulfillment of the prophecy of Isaiah (45:23) on the lordship of the God of Israel over the world. Bending the knee at the name of Jesus, the Church brings forth the truth; she becomes part of the gesture of the cosmos which renders homage to the Victor and thus places herself on the side of the Victor, so that genuflection is an imitative representation of the attitude of the One Who 'was equal to God' and 'humbled Himself unto death.' " [12]

It is also for this reason that it is entirely appropriate to maintain the practice of kneeling to receive Holy Communion. For further confirmation of this position, let us listen to the Holy Father in another passage from *Sacramentum Caritatis*:

"As Saint Augustine put it: 'nemo autem illam carnem manducat, nisi prius adoraverit; peccemus non adorando' – no one eats that flesh without first adoring it; we should sin were we not to adore it. In the Eucharist, the Son of God comes to meet us and desires to become one with us; Eucharistic adoration is simply the natural consequence of the Eucharistic celebration, which is itself the Church's supreme act of adoration. Receiving the Eucharist means adoring Him Whom we receive. Only in this way do we become one with Him, and are given, as it were, a fore-taste of the beauty of the Heavenly Liturgy" (no. 66).

Can we not, then, speak in this regard of a con-tradiction as regards moving forward in procession, as a sign of a people that turns toward her Lord? The Church that, in her external movement, processes and turns toward the Lord is the same Church that, always externally and symbolically, kneels and adores in His Presence. Once again, we are not dealing here with one view to the exclusion of all others, but with a great richness that results from complemen-tary views.

In light of this passage, we can also understand the reason why Pope Benedict XVI, on the occasion of the Solemnity of the Body and Blood of the Lord in 2008, began to distribute Holy Communion to the faithful while they knelt.

Chant and Music

I would like to begin this section with a citation from Pope Saint Gregory the Great, in which we find formulated, with singular depth and force, the central nucleus of music and singing in the liturgy:

"For the voice of melody, whenever it is moved by the intention of the heart, is made thereby to return again to the heart by the agency of Almighty God, so that it pours the mysteries of prophecy or the grace of compunction into the intent mind. Whence it is written: 'The sacrifice of praise shall glorify me: and there is the way by which I will show him the salvation of God' (Ps 49:23). As in the Latin *salutare*, so in Hebrew, Jesus is meant. Furthermore, the way of revelation of Christ is in the sacrifice of praise, because while compunction is poured out through the melody, a way is opened in our hearts whereby we can finally approach Christ, as He speaks of the revelation of Himself" (*In Ez. hom.* 1, 15).

Thus, singing and music in the liturgy, when they are truly themselves, are born from a heart that searches after the mystery of God and become an exegesis of this same mystery, a word that, in musical notation, opens onto the horizon of Christ's salvation. Therefore, there is an intrinsic bond among word, music, and chant in the liturgical celebration. Music and chant, in fact, cannot be separated from the Word of God, of which, indeed, music and chant ought to be a faithful interpretation and revelation. Chant and music in the liturgy stem from the depth of the heart, that is, from Christ Who dwells therein – and they return to the heart, that is, to Christ. And from the question of the heart, He comes as the true and definitive response. This objectivity of chant and liturgical music should never be consigned to the superficial and extemporaneous nature of our sentiments and fleeting emotions, which do not correspond to the greatness of the mystery being celebrated.

And so, it is right to affirm that chant and music

in the liturgy are born from prayer and lead to prayer. Therefore, they permit us to enter into the mystery — to return to the terminology that is part of the title of this Conference. And here, in chant and in music, we find perhaps one of the highest ways by which we enter and participate in the mystery, capable of making a synthesis of so many components of liturgical participation.

Speaking of chant and of music: here permit me to mention briefly the Latin language, in which we find an extraordinary treasure of chant and liturgical music handed down to us from centuries past — a treasure the Church has defined as perennially valid, in and of itself; it is also a criterion for establishing what can be considered truly liturgical in new musical forms that continue to develop in the course of time. I am referring here to Gregorian Chant and to sacred, classical polyphony, forms of liturgical music to be appreciated, today as yesterday, because they are proper to the liturgy and have both artistic value and religious content, and thus should have a place in the liturgical celebration. The perennial value of Gregorian Chant and classical polyphony consists in their capacity to interpret the Word of God and, therefore, the mystery being celebrated and of being at the service of the liturgy — without making the liturgy something that merely serves music and singing. Can we give up the preservation of such treasures that centuries of Church history have handed down to us? Can we cease to draw today from that extraordinary patrimony of spirituality? How will it ever be possible to give flesh to a wider and more worthy repertoire of singing and music, if we do not allow ourselves to be educated by what inspires?

And so, that is one reason to preserve dutifully the use of Latin – without forgetting also the other aspects of this liturgical language, expressive of the universality and catholicity of the Church, which cannot be justifiably set aside. In this regard, how can we not feel an extraordinary experience of the catholicity of the Church when, in Saint Peter's Basilica, men and women of all continents, nationalities, and different languages pray and sing together in the same language? Who does not perceive a warm welcome of a common home when, entering a church in a foreign land, one can unite himself to brethren in the faith through the use of the same language (at least in some parts)?

So that this may continue to be concretely possible, it is necessary that the use of Latin be preserved in our churches and communities with the requisite pastoral wisdom.

4. Conclusion

As I have said, in considering certain aspects related to liturgical celebration, some priority must be followed. To underscore some priorities, to place in the light some problems, to look toward some possible changes — these come from a desire to make a contribution to the full and authentic realization of the liturgical reform undertaken at the Second Vatican Council. For all of us, that reform was and is providential in the historic path of the Church, which develops and grows according to a logic of organic continuity with her past. But precisely because we desire that the carrying out of such a reform would produce all its desired effects, it is also right to examine the problems that have arisen in the course of time from certain not always felicitous assertions and from other concrete realizations not always truly inspired. True fidelity to the reform willed by Vatican II demands that while we promote all that is a true gift of renewal, we take into account existing problems with freedom of spirit, an ecclesial spirit, and without ideologically preconceived notions. It is one and the same love that must animate everyone — love for the Lord and His Church, love for the liturgy, which is the action of Christ and the Church.

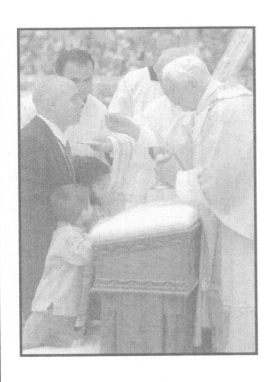

HOLY COMMUNION

HOLY COMMUNION
RECEIVED ON THE TONGUE
AND WHILE KNEELING

The most ancient practice of distributing Holy Communion was, with all probability, to give Communion to the faithful in the palm of the hand. The history of the liturgy, however, makes clear that, rather early on, a process took place to change this practice.

From the time of the Fathers of the Church, a tendency was born and consolidated whereby distribution of Holy Communion in the hand became more and more restricted in favor of distributing Holy Communion on the tongue. The motivation for this practice is twofold: first, to avoid, as much as possible, the dropping of Eucharistic particles; second, to increase among the faithful, devotion to the Real Presence of Christ in the Sacrament of the Eucharist.

Saint Thomas Aquinas also refers to the practice of receiving Holy Communion only on the tongue. He affirms that touching the Body of the Lord is proper only to the ordained priest.

Therefore, for various reasons, among which the Angelic Doctor cites respect for the Sacrament, he writes: ". . . out of reverence towards this Sacrament, nothing touches it, but what is consecrated;

hence the corporal and the chalice are consecrated, and likewise the priest's hands, for touching this Sacrament. Hence, it is not lawful for anyone else to touch it except from necessity, for instance, if it were to fall upon the ground, or else in some other case of urgency" (*Summa Theologiae*, III, 82, 3).

Over the centuries the Church has always characterized the moment of Holy Communion with sacredness and the greatest respect, forcing herself constantly to develop to the best of her ability external signs that would promote understanding of this great sacramental mystery. In her loving and pastoral solicitude the Church has made sure that the faithful receive Holy Communion having the right interior dispositions, among which dispositions stands out the need for the Faithful to comprehend and consider interiorly the Real Presence of Him Whom they are to receive. (See *The Catechism of Pope Pius X*, nos. 628 & 636.) The Western Church has established kneeling as one of the signs of devotion appropriate to communicants. A celebrated saying of Saint Augustine, cited by Pope Benedict XVI in his Encyclical *Sacramentum Caritatis* (Sacrament of Love, no. 66), teaches: "No one eats that flesh without first adoring it; we should sin were we not to adore it" (*Enarrationes in Psalmos* 98, 9). Kneeling indicates and promotes the adoration necessary before receiving the Eucharistic Christ.

From this perspective, the then-Cardinal Ratzinger affirmed that: "Communion reaches its true depth only when it is supported and surrounded by adoration." [13] For this reason, Cardinal Ratzinger maintained that "the practice of kneeling for Holy Communion has in its favor a centuries-old tradition, and it is a particularly expressive sign of adoration, completely appropriate in light of the true, real, and substantial presence of Our Lord Jesus Christ under the consecrated species." [14]

John Paul II, in his last Encyclical, *Ecclesia de Eucharistia* (The Church Comes from the Eucharist), wrote: "By giving the Eucharist the prominence it deserves, and by being careful not to diminish any of its dimensions or demands, we show that we are truly conscious of the greatness of this gift. We are urged to do so by an uninterrupted tradition, which from the first centuries on has found the Christian community ever vigilant in guarding this 'treasure.' Inspired by love, the Church is anxious to hand on to future generations of Christians, without loss, her faith and teaching with regard to the mystery of the Eucharist. There can be no danger of excess in our care for this mystery, for 'in this sacrament is recapitulated the whole mystery of our salvation'" (no. 61).

In continuity with the teaching of his Predecessor, starting with the Solemnity of Corpus Christi in the year 2008, the Holy Father, Benedict XVI, began to distribute to the faithful the Body of the Lord, by placing it directly on the tongue as they remain kneeling.

THE PALLIUM

THE PALLIUM

Among the liturgical insignia of the Supreme Pontiff, one of the more evocative is the pallium, made of white wool, symbol of the bishop as the good shepherd and, at the same time, of the Lamb Crucified for the salvation of the human race. As Pope Benedict XVI made reference to it in his homily for the Holy Mass inaugurating his Petrine ministry on 24 April 2005:

"The symbolism of the pallium is even more concrete: the lamb's wool is meant to represent the lost, sick, or weak sheep which the shepherd places on his shoulders and carries to the waters of life."

The first historical notes about the pallium emerge in Christian antiquity. The *Liber Pontificalis* (Pontifical Book) notes that Pope St. Mark (d. 336) conferred the pallium on the Suburbicarian Bishop of Ostia, one of the consecrators of the Roman Pontiff. Even if we cannot be sure of the historic value of this information, at least it reflects the practice of the fifth and sixth centuries, when the *Liber Pontificalis* was compiled in the ambit of the Roman Curia.

In 513, Pope Symmachus granted the privilege of the pallium to St. Caesarius of Arles; and thereafter the concession of the pallium by the Pope to the bishops of Italy and outside Italy multiplied. In other churches of the West, the pallium used as episcopal insignia was not in evidence, if it was not being granted to the bishops by the Roman Pontiff.

The pallium is the symbol of a special relationship with the Pope and expresses also the power, that, in communion with the Church of Rome, the metropolitan acquires by right in his own jurisdiction. According to Canon Law, a metropolitan must request the pallium within three months of his appointment and may wear it only in the territory of his own diocese and in the other dioceses of his ecclesiastical province (canon 437).

The homophorion, as a liturgical vestment used by Orthodox bishops and Eastern Catholic bishops of the Byzantine Rite, consists of a sash of white material, curved at its center so as to allow it to fit around the neck and to rest on the shoulders, causing the ends to fall onto the chest. In the Eastern tradition, the "great homophorion" (to be distinguished from the smaller version worn by bishops on certain occasions and similar to the *epitrachelion*, which corresponds to the Western stole) has undergone a certain development and today is wider and more ornate in style. Unlike the pallium, the *homophorion* is not reserved for metropolitan archbishops, but can be worn by all bishops.

The liturgical pallium in the most ancient depictions appears in the form of an open scarf placed over the shoulders. In this form we see it in the figure of Archbishop Maximian (498–556) in the Church of San Vitale in Ravenna (which dates to the first half of the sixth century). A strip of the pallium is marked with a cross that hangs in front on the left shoulder, turns around the neck and, passing onto the right shoulder, descends very low toward the chest, to return to the left shoulder and to fall again around the back. This manner of wearing the pallium was maintained until the High Middle Ages when, with the use of pins, it began to be worn so that the two ends hung exactly in the middle of the chest and the back. With the pins replaced by a fixed piece of sewn material, the papal pallium took on the form of an enclosed circle, which one finds commonplace after the ninth century, as in depictions in various Roman basilicas, such as Santa Maria Antiqua, Santa Maria in Trastevere, and San Clemente. The two ends of the pallium, however, always maintained a considerable length, until, after the fifteenth century, they were progressively shortened.

The ornamentation of the pallium, such as one finds illustrated already in a Ravenna mosaic, became thereafter always more elaborate. Four, six, or eight red or black crosses were sewn onto it; on the edge, fringe was sometimes attached. In the developed form of the pallium, the strips end with little bands of lead covered with black silk. The three jeweled pins that originally served to hold the pallium firmly in place, had already, by the thirteenth century, become simply a decorative element.

The long pallium crossed over the left shoulder was not worn by the Pope and the bishops in the West after the Carolingian period. It would seem as though, already in the Middle Ages, one finds a consciousness of this historic development: an illustration of a manuscript from the eleventh century shows St. Gregory the Great wearing the pallium in the contemporary fashion, with the ends falling in the middle, and the Apostle Peter wearing it in the ancient style, on the left shoulder (Library of the Abbey of Montecassino, 73DD). Therefore, the well-known picture located in the Sacro Speco of Subiaco, dating to around 1219 and depicting Pope Innocent III with the ancient type of pallium, seems to be a conscious "archaism."

After having used a pallium that was larger and that crossed over the left shoulder, Benedict XVI began to use again, beginning on the Solemnity of Saints Peter and Paul in 2008, the form of the pallium that had been used until the time of John Paul II, although of a wider and larger style, and with red crosses. The use of this form of the pallium is meant to underscore better the continuous development that this liturgical vestment has known in the span of more than twelve centuries.

The pallium of the metropolitan archbishops, in

its present form, is a straight sash of material of almost five centimeters, made of white wool, curved at the center, thus allowing it to rest on the shoulders over the Roman or Gothic chasuble, and with two black flaps falling in front and behind, so that, seen either from the front or from behind, the vestment reminds one of the letter "Y." It is decorated with six crosses of black silk, one on each end and four on the curve at the shoulders, and is decorated in front and on the back with three pins made of gold and jewels (*acicula*). The different form of the papal pallium compared with that of the metropolitans makes clear the diversity of jurisdiction signified by the pallium.

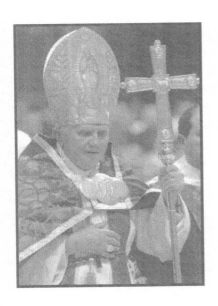

THE STAFF

THE STAFF

The staff [15] as the liturgical insignia of bishops and abbots goes back to the seventh century according to some Spanish sources, although its use could perhaps be older. It seems as though the staff as a symbol of episcopal authority would have passed from the Iberian Peninsula to England, to Gaul, to Germany. However, from the descriptions of the Solemn Papal Mass in the *Ordines Romani* (Roman Ordinals), its use is not mentioned. The portraits of the popes also confirm that the episcopal staff was not part of the papal insignia, because one does not see it in any iconographic artifact made in Rome. Therefore, Pope Innocent III (d. 1216) writes in his *De Sacro altaris mysterio* (Concerning the Sacred Mystery of the Altar, 1.62): "The Roman Pontiff does not use the shepherd's staff."

The reason why the pope did not use the staff resides in the fact that the staff was a symbol of investiture of a newly elected bishop given to him by the metropolitan archbishop or by another bishop (a ceremony which from the Carolingian period until the time of the investiture controversy was conducted increasingly by secular rulers). The pope, however, did not receive investiture from another bishop, as Bernardo Botono of Parma (d. 1263) pointed out in his *Glossa Ordinaria dei Decretali di Gregorio IX* (The Ordinary Glosses of the Decrees of Gregory IX, 15): "The pope receives his power from God alone." Saint Thomas Aquinas offers a further reason, when he comments that: "The Roman Pontiff does not use the staff . . . since it is a sign of limited power, which the curvature of the staff signifies" (*Super Sent.*, lib. 4, d. 24, q. 3, a. 3 ad 8). Here, Saint Thomas refers to the form of the staff hitherto commonplace: one that was twisted at the top, as a sign of pastoral care and jurisdiction.

From the High Middle Ages, if not even before, the popes used a pontifical staff as insignia to signify their temporal power. The precise form of the staff is not well known. It probably was a stick with a cross at the top. In the Middle Ages, after the pope was elected and took possession of the Lateran Basilica, he was presented with the staff by the Prior of Saint Lawrence at the Lateran (the "Holy of Holies") as a "*signum regiminis et correctionis*," that is, as a symbol of his governance, which included the power to mete out punishment and impose penances. The presentation of the staff was an important act, but did not have the same significance as the imposition of the pallium, which took place during the papal coronation ceremony. In fact, the former ceremony was no longer observed from the beginning of the fifteenth century.

The use of the staff was never a part of the papal liturgy, except on some occasions such as the opening of the Holy Door and the consecration of churches, during which the pope took hold of the staff to knock on the door three times and to trace the Greek and Latin letters on the floor of the church. In the late Middle Ages, the popes also used as a staff a crozier with a triple cross.

After Pope Paul VI's election in 1963, he commissioned a Neopolitan sculptor by the name of Lello Scorzelli to design a pastoral staff to be used during solemn liturgical celebrations. This silver crozier went back to the traditional type of staff that took the form of a cross, accompanied, however, by the corpus of the Crucified One. Paul VI used this crozier for the first time for the closing of the Second Vatican Council, on 8 December 1965. Afterward, he made the same use of this crozier – often but not always in liturgical celebrations – as any bishop makes of his crozier. On certain occasions, Paul VI and John Paul II also used the triple cross as insignia.

On Palm Sunday 2008, Pope Benedict XVI substituted this staff, used also by Pope John Paul I, Pope John Paul II, and by himself, with a staff surmounted by a gold cross, which had been given as a gift to Blessed Pope Pius IX in 1877, by the Circolo San Pietro, on the occasion of the fiftieth anniversary of his episcopal consecration.

This crozier had already been used by Blessed Pope John XXIII for various liturgical celebrations during Vatican II.

With the celebration of First Vespers for Advent 2009, the Holy Father, Benedict XVI, began to use a new staff, given to him by the Circolo San Pietro, similar in style to that of Pius IX.

THE CRUCIFIX

THE CRUCIFIX
AT THE CENTER OF THE ALTAR

The Compendium of the *Catechism of the Catholic Church* asks the question: "What is the liturgy?" – and answers:

"The liturgy is the celebration of the mystery of Christ and in particular his paschal mystery. Through the exercise of the priestly office of Jesus Christ, the liturgy manifests in signs and brings about the sanctification of humankind. The public worship which is due to God is offered by the Mystical Body of Christ, that is, by its head and by its members" (no. 218).

From this definition, one understands that Christ the Eternal High Priest – and the Paschal Mystery of His Passion, Death, and Resurrection – is at the center of the liturgical action of the Church. The liturgy must be the celebrated transparency of this theological truth. For many centuries, the sign chosen by the Church to orient the heart and the body during the liturgy has been the depiction of the Crucified Jesus.

The centrality of the crucifix in the celebration of divine worship was more evident in the past, when the normative custom was that both priests and faithful would turn and face the crucifix during the eucharistic celebration. The cross was placed in the center above the altar, which in turn was attached to the wall, according to the norm. For the present custom of celebrating the Eucharist "facing the people," often the crucifix is located to the side of the altar, thus losing its central position.

Then-theologian and Cardinal Joseph Ratzinger many times had underscored that, even during the celebration "facing the people," the crucifix should maintain its central position, and that it would be impossible to think that the depiction of the Crucified Lord – which expresses His Sacrifice and therefore the most important significance of the Eucharist – could be in some way a source of disturbance. Having become Pope, Benedict XVI, in the preface to the first volume of his *Gesammelte Schriften*, said that he was happy about the fact that the proposal he had advanced in his celebrated essay, "The Spirit of the Liturgy," was making headway. That proposal consisted in the suggestion that: "Where a direct common turning toward the east is not possible, the cross can serve as the interior 'east' of faith. It should stand in the middle of the altar and be the common point of focus for both priest and praying community." [16]

The crucifix at the center of the altar recalls many splendid meanings of the Sacred Liturgy, which can be summarized by referring to paragraph 618 of the *Catechism of the Catholic Church* – a passage which concludes with a beautiful citation from St. Rose of Lima:

"The cross is the unique sacrifice of Christ, the 'one mediator between God and men' (1 Tim 2:5). But because in his incarnate divine person he has in some way united himself to every man, 'the possibility of being made partners, in a way known to God, in the paschal mystery' is offered to all men (*Gaudium et Spes*, no. 22). He calls his disciples to 'take up [their] cross and follow [him]' (Mt 16:24), for 'Christ also suffered for [us], leaving [us] an example so that [we] should follow in his steps' (1 Pt 2:21). In fact, Jesus desires to associate with his redeeming sacrifice those who were to be its first beneficiaries (cf. Mk 10:39; Jn 21:18–19; Col 1:24). This is achieved supremely in the case of his mother, who was associated more intimately than any other person in the mystery of his redemptive suffering (cf. Lk 2:35). 'Apart from the cross, there is no other ladder by which we may get to heaven' (St. Rose of Lima, in P. Hansen, *Vita Mirabilis* [Louvain, 1668])."

THE GREEK GOSPEL

CHANTING
OF THE GOSPEL
IN GREEK
IN CERTAIN PAPAL CELEBRATIONS

As has been noted, in the worship of the early Christians there were present: preaching, the reading of Sacred Scripture, prayers, and hymns for a didactic purpose.

In the year 150, Saint Justin, in his *Apology* and in his *Dialogue with Trypho*, gave the first description of the Roman Mass, divided into two parts: the "didactic" part, made up of readings from the Prophets and the Apostles, and the "sacrificial" part, focused on the Passion of the Lord.

Greek was used in the liturgy; the use of Latin came in toward the fourth century; before the fourth century, here and there, the readings were customarily read in Greek, and afterward translated into Latin; thus an almost bi-lingual Mass existed. The custom of proclaiming the readings of the Mass in Greek seems simply to have originated from the need to promote participation among those faithful who could not yet understand Latin.

Nevertheless, the on-going development of the

primacy of the Bishop of Rome, from the time of Saint Ignatius of Antioch, who, in the second century, defines the Church of the City of Rome as the Church that "presides in charity," and says likewise that the universal Church is an organic body built on mutual charity, will have an influence on the preservation of certain parts of the papal liturgy in Greek – an indication of the Pope's solicitude for all the churches, in particular the Eastern Churches. For example, still today in the Roman Liturgy of Good Friday, one sings the Greek chant known as the *Trisagion*, addressed to the Lord Jesus Christ, Who is thrice-holy, because He is God, the Strong One, the Immortal One, and has mercy on us.

After the schism of 1054 between Rome and Constantinople, the longing for the restoration of unity did not die out; rather, the Supreme Pontiff did not give up the intention of reestablishing the communion of the Eastern Churches with the Apostolic See: one thinks of the Council of Florence and of the establishment in Rome, afterward, of the Greek College in 1577 by Pope Gregory XIII. One recalls the institution of the Greek College because this act had its effects, in a certain sense, on the rite of proclaiming the readings in Greek and then in Latin translation. In fact, it was from the Greek College that the Papal Master of Ceremonies used to draw to conduct a bilingual liturgical service.

The following detailed description of the rite of

proclaiming the Epistle and Gospel in Greek and in Latin in the papal liturgy goes back to the beginning of the twentieth century:

The Apostolic Subdeacon takes from one of the Clerics of the Pontifical Chapel the Epistle Book, and having made a genuflection to the altar and to the Supreme Pontiff, with the assistance of a Pontifical Master of Ceremonies, goes to the far end of the pew, in which the Cardinal Priests are seated, waits until all are seated, and at the sign from the Master of Ceremonies chants the Epistle. He remains there for the duration of the Epistle chanted in Greek. The Epistle having been chanted in Latin, the Subdeacon of the Greek Rite takes from another Cleric of the Pontifical Chapel the Greek Epistle Book, and having carried out the same ceremonies, and assisted by another Pontifical Master of Ceremonies, chants the Epistle next to the Apostolic Subdeacon.

After the chanting of the Epistle in Greek, the Apostolic Subdeacon and that of the Greek Rite, guided by the Pontifical Masters of Ceremonies, go to the papal throne, and having made a genuflection, go up, kissing, one after the other, the foot of the Pontiff; then the deacons genuflect to the Pope and return to the altar, where each one genuflects to the Cross, and returns the Epistle Book to the Cleric of the Pontifical Chapel.

The Subdeacon of the Greek Rite returns to the column of the altar, to the Epistle side, and the Apostolic Subdeacon stops near the Cardinal Deacon who is ministering, and then reads the Epistle and the Gradual. Two Archbishops assisting at the foot of the throne ascend the papal throne with the Book and with the Candle. The Supreme Pontiff reads the Epistle, the Gradual and the Gospel. When the Supreme Pontiff signs the Gospel, the Cardinal Deacon who is ministering, takes off his miter, descends from the altar, and receives the Gospel Book from the Train-bearer. The Cardinal Deacon then, having made the prescribed bows, places the Gospel Book on the altar, and remains near the altar, until the Pope has finished reading. Afterward the Cardinal Deacon approaches the papal throne, to kiss the hand of the Holy Father.

At the same time, a Pontifical Master of Ceremonies leads the Thurifer-Prelate, who holds the thurible and the boat, to the papal throne, for the imposition of incense. The Cardinal Suburbicarian Bishop holds the boat before the Pope, to whom he offers, with the prescribed kisses, the little spoon, asking the Pope for the blessing of the incense with the usual formula.

The Cardinal Deacon who is ministering, having kissed the hand of the Pope, returns to the altar and, having genuflected on the edge of the predella, says the prayer: *Munda cor meum*, etc.

The Voting Acolytes of the Apostolic Signatura, taking into their hands seven candelabra, stop near the steps leading up to the altar, with the Apostolic Subdeacon standing in their midst.

The Thurifer, with the thurible and the boat, returns to the throne at the altar, and places himself near the Prelates, who carry candles, on the Epistle side.

The Cardinal Deacon who is ministering, having said the *Munda cor meum*, takes the Gospel Book from the middle of the altar, descends from there, and places himself to the right of the Apostolic Subdeacon. All genuflect to the Cross, except for the Cardinal Deacon, who makes a profound bow.

Turning around and turning back afterward, they switch so that the Cardinal Deacon who is ministering, as he proceeds to the throne, is on the right of the Subdeacon, and at the right of the Cardinal are the four Acolytes, while the three others are placed to the left of the Subdeacon.

Having arrived before the steps of the throne, all genuflect, except for the Cardinal Deacon who is ministering, who bowing profoundly toward the Supreme Pontiff, asks for the blessing, saying: *Iube, Domne, benedicere*. The Pope gives him the blessing, responding, *Dominus sit in corde tuo*, etc.

After the Pope has given the blessing, all stand up, and again genuflect, except for the Cardinal Deacon who is ministering, who makes a profound bow. By the shortest route, they proceed, in the same way, from the altar to the throne, near the lectern already prepared by a Cleric of the Pontifical Chapel, near the pew of the Cardinal Deacons, by the altar.

The Thurifer stays with the Pontifical Master of Ceremonies to the left of the lectern, at the back side of which the Apostolic Subdeacon positions himself.

The Prelate Acolytes line up in such a way that four of them are on the right of the lectern and three on the left. The Cardinal Deacon who is ministering stands before the lectern and opens the Gospel Book on it, for the chanting of the Gospel.

Meanwhile, the second Assisting Cardinal Deacon takes the gremial and the miter to the Supreme Pontiff. The Supreme Pontiff rises and remains standing until the chanting of the Gospel has ended.

The Cardinal Deacon who is ministering, sings: *Dominus vobiscum* and then: *Sequentia sancti Evangelii*, etc., signing at the same time the Gospel Book and himself. The Thurifer hands the thurible to the Cardinal Deacon who is ministering, who then incenses the Gospel Book, and afterward returns the thurible to the Thurifer, who remains in the same place, for the chanting of the Gospel in Greek.

The Gospel having been chanted in Greek, the Apostolic Subdeacon takes the Gospel Book and, holding it before his chest, stops at the right of the lectern.

The Pope sits, and the first Assisting Cardinal Deacon hands the miter to the Pope.

Two Acolytes remain *hinc inde* near the lectern, the other five, having made the required genuflections to the Supreme Pontiff and to the altar, while the Cardinal Deacon who is ministering makes a profound bow, they return to the credence table and put down the candelabra.

The Cardinal Deacon who is ministering, goes to sit at the faldstool and puts on his miter. In the meantime, the Deacon of the Greek Rite takes the Gospel Book from a Cleric of the Chapel, and places it on the mensa of the altar, having made genuflections to the Supreme Pontiff and to the Cross.

Afterward, the Cardinal Deacon descends immediately and again genuflects to the Cross, goes to the papal throne, genuflects, and goes up to the top step of the throne to kiss the foot of the Pope. The Cardinal Deacon returns to the altar, and while still kneeling in the middle on the highest step, says the prayer that one usually says before the proclamation of the Gospel.

In the meantime the Subdeacon of the Greek Rite waits before the stairs of the altar, in order to join the Deacon. The Deacon, having said the prayer, takes the Gospel Book, descends from the altar, genuflects to the Cross together with the Subdeacon; and then, accompanied by a Pontifical Master of Ceremonies, both go to the steps leading up to the papal throne. All remain kneeling on the floor before the steps while the Deacon asks for the blessing of the Supreme Pontiff.

Then all rise, genuflect to the Holy Father, and go by the shortest route to the lectern. The Subdeacon places himself at the back of the lectern, and the Deacon at the front of the lectern, opening thereon the Gospel Book.

In the meantime, the second Assisting Cardinal Deacon takes the miter from the Pope, who then stands up and remains standing for the duration of the chanting of the Gospel.

The Cardinal Deacon who ministers takes off the miter, rises, and remains standing before the faldstool.

The Deacon of the Greek Rite begins the chanting of the Gospel, and, with the thurible handed to him by the Thurifer, incenses the Gospel Book. He hands back the thurible and continues the chant until the end. The Subdeacon, with the chanting of the Gospel complete and having said the words *Doxa soi, Kyrie, doxa soi*, takes the Gospel Book, and positions himself to the left of the Apostolic Subdeacon.

The Greek Deacon, flanked by two Acolytes, returns to the Epistle side near the column of the altar. The Acolytes place the candelabra on the credence table. The Apostolic Subdeacon, the Greek Subdeacon (followed by the Thurifer with the thurible, together with a Pontifical Master of Ceremonies) move toward the throne, and one after the other, ascending the throne, without genuflecting, present the Sacred Text to the Supreme Pontiff, who meanwhile kisses it and repeats the words: *Per evangelica dicta*, etc.

Both Subdeacons descend from the throne, genuflect to the Supreme Pontiff, and return to the altar. Having made a genuflection near the steps, each one hands over his respective Gospel Book to the Cleric of the Pontifical Chapel. The Apostolic Subdeacon positions himself near the Cardinal Deacon who is ministering; the Greek Subdeacon joins the Greek Deacon near the column of the altar, on the Epistle side.

The Assisting Cardinal Bishop, guided by the Master of Ceremonies, after the Pope has kissed the Sacred Text of the Gospels in Latin and in Greek, descends onto a step, and, having received the thurible from the Thurifer, incenses the Supreme Pontiff with a triple swing, returning the thurible to the Voting Member of the Signatura who, having genuflected to the Pope and the altar, gives it to the Acolyte of the Pontifical Chapel. [17]

In conclusion, without any pretense of our having treated this topic in an exhaustive manner, one can hold that the present practice of chanting the Gospel in Greek during the *Liturgia Verbi*, as well as that of the diptychs of the Anaphora, has solid historical and theological foundations, reminding one of the interdependent relationship between the *lex credendi* and the *lex orandi* in the Christian liturgy. Besides, this practice of chanting the Gospel in both Latin and Greek is always a manifestation of the sole Catholic Church, even when the liturgy is celebrated in a particular community. The Roman Liturgy, specifically, manifests the Catholic ecclesiology which recognizes the Bishop of Rome as the universal pastor.

SILENCE

PERIODS OF SILENCE
WITHIN THE
EUCHARISTIC CELEBRATION

The General Instruction of the Roman Missal (third and emended typical edition, 2008) prescribes:

"Sacred silence also, as part of the celebration, is to be observed at the designated times. Its purpose, however, depends on the time it occurs in each part of the celebration. Thus within the Act of Penitence and again after the invitation to pray, all recollect themselves; but at the conclusion of a reading or the homily, all meditate briefly on what they have heard; then, after Communion, they praise and pray to God in their hearts. Even before the celebration itself, it is commendable that silence be observed in the church, in the sacristy, in the vesting room, and in adjacent areas, so that all may dispose themselves to carry out the sacred action in a devout and fitting manner" (no. 45).

The liturgy Constitution *Sacrosanctum Concilium* likewise prescribes: "And at the proper times all should observe a reverent silence" (no. 30).

The General Instruction specifies better the importance of silence within the Liturgy of the Word (no. 56), while it makes the same clear for the

Liturgy of the Eucharist: "The Eucharistic Prayer demands that all listen to it with reverence and in silence" (no. 78); then underscores the importance of the observance of silence as a means of good preparation for the reception of Holy Communion: "The priest prepares himself by a prayer, said quietly, that he may fruitfully receive Christ's Body and Blood. The faithful do the same, praying silently" (no. 84). Finally, the same attitude is proposed for the period of thanksgiving after Communion:

"When the distribution of Communion is finished, as circumstances suggest, the priest and faithful spend some time praying privately.[18] If desired, a psalm or other canticle of praise or a hymn may also be sung by the entire congregation" (no. 88).

In several other paragraphs of the General Instruction similar directives concerning silence are repeated, such that silence is an integral part of the liturgical celebration.

The Servant of God John Paul II had recognized that, in actual practice, the directive of the Second Vatican Council concerning sacred silence, a directive later included in the General Instruction, was not always faithfully observed. He writes: "One aspect that we must foster in our communities with greater commitment is *the experience of silence.* . . . The liturgy, with its different moments and symbols, cannot ignore silence" (*Spiritus et Sponsa*, no. 13).

Here we can recall a text of the then-theologian and Cardinal Joseph Ratzinger:

"We are realizing more and more clearly that silence is part of the liturgy. We respond, by singing and praying, to the God Who addresses us, but the greater mystery, surpassing all words, summons us to silence. It must, of course, be a silence with content, not just the absence of speech and action. We should expect the liturgy to give us a positive stillness that will restore us." [19]

Consequently, the observance of the moments of silence envisioned by the liturgy is of great importance. These moments of silence are as much an integral part of the *ars celebrandi* (art of celebrating) of the ministers as is *participatio actuosa* (active participation) on the part of the faithful. Silence in the liturgy is the moment in which one listens with greater attention to the voice of God and internalizes His word, so that it bears the fruit of sanctity in daily life.

LATIN

THE LATIN LANGUAGE

Undoubtedly, Latin is the language that has the most longevity in the Roman Liturgy: It has been in use now for more than sixteen centuries, that is to say, from the time when the official liturgical language of the Church went from Greek to Latin – a change completed under Pope Damasus (d. 384). The official liturgical books of the Roman Rite are still published in Latin today (*editio typica*).

The Code of Canon Law stipulates: "The eucharistic celebration is to be carried out in the Latin language or in another language provided that the liturgical texts have been legitimately approved" (can. 928). Taking into consideration the present situation, this canon translates in a concise manner the teaching of the Constitution of the Sacred Liturgy of the Second Vatican Council.

The well-known number 36 of *Sacrosanctum Concilium* established the following principle:

"Particular law remaining in force, the use of the Latin language is to be preserved in the Latin rites"(§ 1).

In this sense, the Code affirms first of all: "The eucharistic celebration is to be carried out in the Latin language."

In the sections which follow, *Sacrosanctum Concilium* admits of the possibility of using also the vernacular languages:

"But since the use of the mother tongue, whether in the Mass, the administration of the sacraments, or other parts of the liturgy, frequently may be of great advantage to the people, the limits of its employment may be extended. This will apply in the first place to the readings and directives, and to some of the prayers and chants, according to the regulations on this matter to be laid down separately in subsequent chapters" (§ 2).

"These norms being observed, it is for the competent territorial ecclesiastical authority mentioned in Article 22.2, to decide whether, and to what extent, the vernacular language is to be used; their decrees are to be approved, that is, confirmed, by the Apostolic See. And, whenever it seems to be called for, this authority is to consult with bishops of neighboring regions which have the same language" (§ 3).

"Translations from the Latin text into the mother tongue intended for use in the liturgy must be approved by the competent territorial ecclesiastical authority mentioned above" (§ 4).

On the basis of those subsequent sections, the

Code adds: "or in another language provided that the liturgical texts have been legitimately approved."

As can be seen, likewise according to present norms, the Latin language still holds primacy of place as that language which, based on principle, the Church prefers, even though she recognizes that the vernacular can be useful for the faithful. In the present concrete situation, liturgical celebrations in Latin have become rather rare. Hence, there is a motivation for using Latin inasmuch as, in the Papal liturgy (but not only in the papal liturgy), Latin should be safeguarded as a precious inheritance of the Western liturgical tradition. Not by chance did the Servant of God John Paul II recall that:

"The Roman Church has special obligations towards Latin, the splendid language of ancient Rome, and she must manifest them whenever the occasion presents itself" (*Dominicae cenae*, no. 10).

In continuity with the Magisterium of his Predecessor, Pope Benedict XVI, besides wishing that there would be a greater use of the traditional Latin language in liturgical celebrations, especially during international gatherings, wrote:

"Speaking more generally, I ask that future priests, from their time in the seminary, receive the preparation needed to understand and to celebrate Mass in Latin, and also to use Latin texts and execute Gregorian chant; nor should we forget that the faithful can be taught to recite the more common prayers in Latin, and also to sing parts of the liturgy to Gregorian chant" (*Sacramentum Caritatis*, no. 62).

BEAUTY

BEAUTY
IN EVERY ASPECT OF
THE LITURGICAL RITE

The Holy Father, Benedict XVI, in the Exhortation *Sacramentum Caritatis*, writes:

"This relationship between creed and worship is evidenced in a particular way by the rich theological and liturgical category of beauty. Like the rest of Christian Revelation, the liturgy is inherently linked to beauty: it is *veritatis splendor*. The liturgy is a radiant expression of the paschal mystery, in which Christ draws us to himself and calls us to communion" (no. 35).

The beauty of the liturgy is part of this mystery; it is a sublime expression of God's glory and, in a certain sense, a glimpse of Heaven on earth. The memorial of Jesus' redemptive sacrifice contains something of that beauty which Peter, James, and John beheld when the Master, making His way to Jerusalem, was transfigured before their eyes (cf. Mk 9:2). Beauty, then, is not mere decoration, but rather an essential element of the liturgical action, since it is an attribute of God Himself and His revelation. These considerations should make us realize the care which is needed if the liturgical action is to reflect its innate splendor.

The beauty of Christ is reflected above all in the

saints and in faithful Christians of every age, but one should not forget or underestimate the spiritual value of the works of art that the Christian Faith knew how to produce in order to place them at the service of divine worship. The beauty of the liturgy is manifested concretely through material objects and bodily gestures, of which man – a unity of soul and body – has need to elevate himself toward invisible realities and to be reinforced in his faith. The Council of Trent taught:

"And since the nature of man is such that he cannot without external means be raised easily to meditation on divine things, holy mother Church has instituted certain rites . . . whereby both the majesty of so great a sacrifice might be emphasized and the minds of the faithful excited by those visible signs of religion and piety to the contemplation of those most sublime things which are hidden in this sacrifice" (Denziger-Schönmetzer, no. 1746).

Sacred art, sacred vestments and vessels, sacred architecture – all must come together to consolidate the sense of majesty and beauty, to make transparent the "noble simplicity" (see *Sacrosanctum Concilium*, no. 34) of the Christian liturgy, which is a liturgy of the true Beauty.

The Servant of God John Paul II recalled the Gospel account of the anointing of Jesus at Bethany, in order to respond to the possible objection concerning the beauty of churches and of objects destined for divine worship, which could seem out of place if considered before the great mass of the earth's poor people. He wrote:

"A woman, whom John identifies as Mary the sister of Lazarus, pours a flask of *costly ointment* over Jesus' head, which provokes from the disciples – and from Judas in particular (cf. Mt 26:8; Mk 14:4; Jn 12:4) – an indignant response, as if this act, in light of the needs of the poor, represented an intolerable 'waste.' But Jesus' own reaction is completely different. While in no way detracting from the duty of charity towards the needy, for whom the disciples must always show special care – "the poor you will always have with you" (Mt 26:11; Mk 14:7; cf. Jn 12:8) – he looks towards his imminent death and burial, and sees this act of anointing as an anticipation of the honor which his body will continue to merit even after his death, indissolubly bound as it is to the mystery of his person" (*Ecclesia de Eucharistia*, no. 47).

And he concluded:

"Like the woman who anointed Jesus in Bethany, *the Church has feared no 'extravagance,'* devoting the best of her resources to expressing her wonder and adoration before the *unsurpassable gift of the Eucharist.* . . . With this heightened sense of mystery, we understand how the faith of the Church in the mystery of the Eucharist has found historical expression not only in the demand for an interior disposition of devotion, but also in *outward forms* meant to evoke and emphasize the grandeur of the event being celebrated. . . . On this foundation *a rich artistic heritage* also developed. Architecture, sculpture, painting and music, moved by the Christian mystery, have found in the Eucharist, both directly and indirectly, a source of great inspiration" (nos. 48–49).

Therefore, it is necessary to exhibit all possible care and attention, so that the dignity of the liturgy will shine forth even in the smallest details in the form of true beauty. It is necessary to recall that even those saints who lived poverty with a particular ascetical commitment always desired that the most beautiful and precious objects be used for divine worship. We mention here only one example, that of the Holy Curé d'Ars:

"From the moment he saw it [the parish church of Ars], M. Vianney loved the old church as he had loved the paternal home. When he undertook its restoration he began with what holds the foremost place, the altar, which is the centre and raison d'être of the sanctuary. Out of reverence for the Holy Eucharist, he wished to secure as beautiful an altar as possible. . . . After these improvements, he undertook the task, to use his own picturesque and touching phrase, of adding to the household possessions of the good God – *le ménage du bon Dieu*. He went to Lyons to visit the workshops of embroiderers and goldsmiths. Whatever was most precious he purchased, so that the purveyors of church furniture would say with astonishment: 'In this district there lives a little curé, lean, badly dressed, looking as if he had not a *sou* in his pocket, yet only the very best things are good enough for his church.'" [20]

THE DALMATIC

THE DALMATIC
AND CARDINAL DEACONS

As at Jerusalem, so also in the primitive Roman Church, we find immediately that when Christians became more numerous, seven deacons assisted the Pope in assemblies of the faithful and in the administration and exercise of charity. The *Liber Pontificalis* attributes to Clement I (92–99) the division of Rome into seven regions for the care of the poor of the City, and thus for this service do we find the deacons set apart. As a matter of fact, Clement's successor, Pope Evaristus (99–108), clarified the functions of deacons in the Church and ordained seven deacons to assist the Bishop of Rome in the distribution of alms.

In the third century, Pope Fabian (236–250) better organized the work of the seven deacons, creating fourteen regions in Rome and entrusting two regions to each deacon.

With the growing number of Christians, other priests and deacons were assigned as auxiliaries to the principal titulars of the churches and diaconates (deaneries). In reality, for the service of the Church of Rome, the deacons were not sufficient and therefore Pope Cletus (80–92) established twenty-five as the fixed number of priests, for the service of the

City, with a territory entrusted to each. Thus, parishes began to develop.

During the pontificate of Gregory I (590–604), the number of regions in Rome doubled, and so the number of deacons in Rome became fourteen. During the pontificate of Gregory II (715–731), four new deacons were added. These new deacons were called "palatine" deacons [21] because they were chosen to serve at the Lateran Basilica. Thus, the number of deacons grew to eighteen. The role of these deacons consisted in helping the Pope during the weekday Masses, to which they were assigned according to their turn. In the second half of the eleventh century, with the re-organization of the College of Cardinals, the churches of the diaconates began to be assigned by title to eighteen cardinals. Therefore, these cardinals became known as "cardinal deacons," remaining as such in conjunction with the titles of their respective churches.

One can say that these principal priests and deacons had to help the Pope in the Roman basilicas where they were incardinated, and thus they began to be known as "cardinals." From this moment forward, they came to be called "cardinal priests and deacons," this is to say, "incardinated." At this point, we discover that, from 1150, the Roman presbyterate – counselors and cooperators of the Pope, the Bishop of Rome – began to constitute the College of Cardinals together with their dean (who was the Bishop of Ostia), as well as the camerlengo, who acted as the administrator of papal goods.

Thus we see that from the earliest times cardinal deacons were employed for the administration of the Church of Rome and for the liturgical service of the Pope. And so it would remain for centuries to come. Only in the eleventh century, with the ecclesiastical reform of Pope Leo X, did the cardinals become less tied to the liturgical and pastoral service of the Diocese of Rome, so that they became the direct helpers of the Pope in service to the universal Church.

On the other hand, and in direct relationship to the cardinal deacons, we find the dalmatic. From the beginning of the third century, this vestment had become the outerwear of the most distinguished people of Rome. We find mention of the dalmatic in the *Liber Pontificalis* as a distinctive, honorary garment granted to the Roman deacons by Pope Sylvester (314–335), "so that deacons would use dalmatics in church" (*Liber Pontificalis*, ed. Mommsen 1.1, p. 50) to distinguish them among the clergy because they had a special relationship with the Pope. Before that, the dalmatic was part of the papal wardrobe and the proper and distinctive garb of the bishop. Outside Rome, deacons wore a simple white tunic for liturgical services, over which was soon added the orarium or stole.

The news of the concession of the dalmatic to the deacons by Pope Sylvester is confirmed by the

Roman author of the *Quaestionum Veteris et Novi Testamenti* (circa 370), who, not without a touch of irony, writes: "Today the deacons vest like bishops" (no. 46). This is evidence that the Roman Church retained the use of the dalmatic as its own privilege, and that only the Pope was able to confer it.

The fact that this Roman custom was still in place in the tenth century is affirmed in the *Ordines Romani XXXVI* (no. 26), where the rubric maintains that the prerogative of the dalmatic was for the cardinal deacons, that is, for the seven regional deacons of the Diocese of Rome, who received the dalmatic upon ordination, while the deacons outside the Diocese of Rome were not permitted to use it.

With the establishment of the Roman Liturgy in Gaul (now France) during the Carolingian period, the dalmatic became rather common, although Rome always opposed its use outside the Diocese of Rome. Probably from the eleventh century forward, the dalmatic became the true and proper outer liturgical vestment of deacons, while bishops and priests wore it underneath the chasuble.[22]

From what we have briefly outlined, one can surmise that when cardinal deacons wore the dalmatic to serve the Supreme Pontiff in liturgical celebrations, we are dealing with a typically Roman liturgical usage in strict relation to the history of the Popes and the papal liturgy.

The cardinal deacons wear the dalmatic when they serve the Pope, whether at Mass or in other liturgical celebrations, but not when they concelebrate with him. In this second instance, they wear the vestment proper to each priest who functions as the principal celebrant, which is the Gothic or Roman chasuble.

Wearing the dalmatic when serving the Pope serves in reality to manifest externally their function as "ministers" of the Pope. One should not forget that, as history has shown us, the true significance of the dalmatic does not necessarily suppose that only deacons can use it.

On the other hand, bishops wear the dalmatic on the most solemn occasions, underneath the chasuble, and also as the outer vestment when anointing the altar or during the washing of the feet. In this latter instance, as the *Caeremoniale Episcoporum* (Ceremonial of Bishops, no. 301) relates, the bishop takes off the miter and chasuble but not the dalmatic. The dalmatic underscores not so much the fullness of the priesthood but service as a characteristic of episcopal ministry. In the case of cardinal deacons wearing the dalmatic, this goes to underscore their role as servants and also as close collaborators of the Roman Pontiff in the liturgy. The dalmatic is a sign of service, of dedication to the Gospel and to others. But also, when the bishop uses the dalmatic, he uses it to serve: whether during the washing of the feet, or in the special liturgical service that bishops, who are cardinal deacons, carry out near to the Roman Pontiff.

We can say, then, that the dalmatic used for liturgical service on the part of cardinal deacons has to do with the dynamic of serving the Church, which Pope Benedict XVI invoked in a homily at a consistory for creating new cardinals (24 November 2007):

"Christians are called to assume the condition of a 'servant,' following in Jesus' footsteps, that is, spending their lives for others in a free and disinterested way. It is not the search for power and success but humble self-giving for the good of the Church that must mark our every action and our every word. True Christian greatness, in fact, does not consist in dominating but in serving. Today, Jesus repeats to every one of us that he 'came not to be served but to serve, and to give his life as a ransom for many' (Mk 10:45). This is the ideal that must direct your service. Dear Brothers, on entering the College of Cardinals, the Lord asks of you and entrusts to you the service of love: love for God, love for His Church, love for the brethren with maximum, unconditional dedication, *usque ad sanguinis effusionem*, as is shown by the formula for the conferral of the hat and the red color of the clothes you are wearing."

Notes

1. General Audience, 5 May 2010.

2. Apostolic Letter, *Vicesimus Quintus Annus*, no. 10.

3. 15 April 2010.

4. *Vicesimus Quintus Annus*, no. 25.

5. Address to the Ecclesial Convention of the Diocese of Rome, 15 June 2010.

6. *The Spirit of the Liturgy* (San Francisco: Ignatius Press, 2000), pp. 171–172.

7. *Vicesimus Quintus Annus*, no. 6.

8. *Il Mistero della Chiesa nella Liturgia* (The Mystery of the Church in the Liturgy) (Edizioni San Paolo, 2007), p. 158.

9. Homily for the Celebration of Vespers in the Cathedral of Notre Dame in Paris, 12 September 2008.

10. *Feast of Faith* (San Francisco: Ignatius Press, 1986), pp. 140–145, passim.

11. Op. cit., pp. 174–175.

12. Cited in the Letter "This Congregation" of the Congregation for Divine Worship and the Discipline of the Sacraments, 1 July 2002.

13. *The Spirit of the Liturgy*, p. 90.

14. In the review *Communio* 35 (Italian edition, 1977).

15. It should be noted that while Italian has several names for this liturgical object, each carrying a particular nuance, this variety is not generally available in English. Thus, "crozier" and "pastoral staff" are used interchangeably.

16. *The Spirit of the Liturgy*, p. 83.

17. Giambattista Maria Menghini, *Le Solenni Ceremonie della Messa Pontificale Celebrata dal Sommo Pontefice*, ed. Desclée Lefebvre et al. (Pontifici, Roma 1904), chap. 4, § 3.

18. The original Latin word is *secreto*, which the English here renders as "privately," is better translated as "quietly" or "in silence."

19. *The Spirit of the Liturgy*, p. 209.

20. Abbé Francis Trochu, *The Curé d'Ars* (Westminster, Md.: The Newman Press, 1960), 127.

21. Palatini, because they served the papal *palatium* (palace).

22. Italian uses two different words for the outer garment of priests and bishops at Mass: *pianeta* and *casula*. English has only "chasuble," which is then distinguished by adjectives, such as "Roman" or "fiddle-back" (in colloquial use) for the *pianeta*, and "Gothic" for the *casula*.